# ENDORSEMENTS

I have always stood in awe of Tami's voice as a model and a teacher of mental confidence. She played a major role in my team's two back to back state championships. *The Confident Athlete* is an enormously powerful tool and step by step guide for coaches and athletes at all levels. Tami is an expert at putting athletes and coaches in the ideal state of mind and body that allows great performances to emerge. The knowledge to be gained from this book is fantastic and essential for success!
*-Toni Leopard, former collegiate and high school basketball coach*

Confidence- it's that thing that successful athletes seem to have so much of, and everyone else wants more. Tami teaches that confidence is a skill, and that everyone can have more of it. She has a knack for relating this to athletes of all levels. Use her 4-step process, and you will have a lot of ah-ha moments as your confidence grows!
*-Angie Ridgeway, LPGA Tour Veteran, D1 Golf Coach*

The Confident Athlete should be in the hands of every student, athlete, teacher, coach, mentor and parent. Confidence is a learned behavior and should be integrated early. It took me years through trial and error to find my own. It's a tough road, when you do not have a foundation. This important attribute carries over to every aspect of our life - making friends, dating, marriage, parenting, and your chosen profession. Confidence is critical to navigate through this thing called life and our own unique and personal journey. Here's a thought ~ What if every student graduated from high school with confidence? *-Meri Sanders, non-athlete*

# The Confident Athlete

# 4 Easy Steps to Build & Maintain Confidence

Tami Matheny

**AUTHOR ACADEMY** elite

Paperback ISBN-13:   978-1-64085-170-2
Hardback  ISBN-13:   978-1-64085-171-9


Library of Congress Control Number:   2017917529

# DEDICATION

This book is dedicated to the coaches and athletes I have been blessed to work with. You guys help me have the best job in the world! Thank you for allowing me to do what I love to do and helping me to evolve on this confidence journey. This is for you!

And to my cousin, Chadd Boy, who thought I could do anything. This is for you! You are missed beyond words!

# CONTENTS

Introduction

Chapter1:  Confidence is Talking the Talk

Chapter 2:  Confidence is Walking the Walk

Chapter 3:  Talking the Talk & Walking the Walk

Chapter 4:  Confidence is Seeing It to Be It

Chapter 5:  Confidence is Being Prepared

Chapter 6:  Talk, Walk, See & Prepare

# ACKNOWLEDGEMENTS

As an athlete, my confidence evolved over time. I owe much of this evolution to family members who have always supported my drive in athletics, some tremendous teammates (Christi Cranford- thanks for teaching me the importance of being physically fit), and to my high school coaches (Alan Carver & Dina Smith) who both believed in me even when I didn't.

I also want to thank some very special friends that have helped me on this journey of writing my first book: Maile Kim, Victoria Bennett, Travis Fravel, and several others that wished not to be named- you know who you are though! The encouragement and guidance of my support group has kept this book going even when I was ready to stop writing.

# INTRODUCTION

*"Low self-confidence isn't a life sentence.
Self-confidence can be learned, practiced, and mastered-
just like any other skill. Once you master it,
everything in your life will change for the better..."*
*-Barrie Davenport*

*Jim had just graduated from high school and his family
threw him a graduation party with all his family and
friends in attendance. Jim's rich uncle, Paul, whom he
rarely saw, was at the party as well. After hearing from
Jim's mom that he was an average student, Uncle Paul
thought he would challenge Jim. "Look I hear you did well
enough to get into college but nothing more. What are your
goals in college?"*

*Jim thought for a second and said, "Pretty much the
same. I'll do enough to graduate." "Tell you what. Do more
than enough. Graduate highest of honors and do it in 4
years, and I'll buy you anything you want."*

*Jim thought for a second how that didn't sound like much
fun, but he said, "Ok. If I do that I'll take a car."*

"I'm serious and I want you to take this seriously too. What kind of car?" Jim didn't even have a car, so any would have been a step up, but he looked out at his uncle's $85,000 sports car and said, "a brand new one like yours."

"Deal. If you do this, I'll be back for your college graduation party with a brand-new sports car."

To make a long story short, Jim went off to college and had his priorities straight. He started taking school seriously, which he had never done before. Every time he felt like sleeping late, he got up early. Every time he felt like cutting class, he went to class. He didn't allow himself to hang out with friends until all work was complete. At the end of the four years, he graduated top of his class.

The night Jim graduated his parents threw a party for him. Everyone was there except his uncle, and no car. Jim was a little bummed and disappointed in his uncle. After the party it was getting late, so he started to help his mom clean up. Jim took the trash to the garage and there it was - a brand new red $85,000 sports car.

Even though it was late, Jim drove over and picked up his best friend Ray. They went to a drag strip-like straight away, where the police never go, so they could see how fast the car could go.

Jim got the car up to 100 mph. Ray said, "Come on. This car is built to go faster than this." Jim stepped on the gas, but *he still couldn't get the car to go over 100 mph. Ray jumped out of the passenger seat and said "Move over. Let me show you what this car is meant to do."*

*He got behind the wheel and.... still the odometer said 100 mph. A little embarrassed, he said, "something is wrong with this car. It should be able to go much faster than this. You'd better take it back to the dealer tomorrow."*

*When Jim drove into the dealership the next day, he was greeted by the dealer. When the dealer heard the problem, he said he would have his mechanic check it out. The mechanic came back in about 5 minutes tops. He whispered in the dealer's ear. He smiled and turned to Jim and said, "You're the kid who got all A's in college, aren't you?" Jim nodded.*

*"How long have you been driving?"*

*"Five years."*

*"Let's see if I got this right. You've been driving for five years and you're smart enough to get all A's in college, but you don't know that you don't drive a $85,000 sports car with the emergency brake on?" (Author Unknown)*

\*\*\*

How many of us have our emergency brake on? We are operating pretty efficiently, but have we reached our potential? Most of us aren't running and performing to the level we were made to. What I have come to realize is that the majority of emergency brakes boil down to confidence: either a lack of confidence or roller coaster confidence (full of confidence when things go your way and then a loss of confidence when things aren't going well).

My goal for this book is to help you release your confidence emergency brake; to give you tools that will allow you to perform with the highest level of confidence. I will discuss the 4 basic building blocks for confidence and give exercises with each one to assist you in releasing your confidence emergency brake.

Confidence seems to be this elusive "thing" that athletes either have or don't have, or sometimes they have and sometimes they don't. Confidence can seem like the hardest thing in the world to regain after a bad performance or after a series of misfortunes. However, if you **consistently** apply the techniques outlined in this book, you will have a steady supply of confidence, enabling you to get off the confidence roller-coaster.

How many of you work at your sport almost every day? How many of you work on fitness consistently? Why? To get better right? So, how many of you work on building or maintaining your confidence? Confidence is a way to improve your game without additional physical work.

And if you commit to working on it, I promise you will see an increase in your game. I don't have the magical pill that everyone wants but I do have a game plan that, if followed, will increase your confidence.

**Note:** *The ideas I have outlined in the book are specified toward athletics but can be applied to any area in life.*

***

## Common Confidence Mistakes:

### 1. *Confidence is something you are either born with or without.*

> Many think if someone has confidence, they were born with it. However, confidence is an acquired skill just like throwing a ball, shooting a ball, swinging a club, etc. are acquired skills. Confidence is more like a job, than a gift you are born with. Most athletes simply do not think of confidence building as something they can work productively towards. Once you accept that it is, the rest becomes easier. Realizing that you can improve confidence through practice and repetition, just as you would other skills, gives you the power to do something about it.

**2.** *If you are already confident, you don't need to work at it.*

A big mistake athletes often make is thinking that they don't need to work on their confidence if they are already at a high level. Yet, you don't stop working out in the weight room just because you are strong; you continue to build more muscle. The same is true with confidence. Even if you have a steady supply of it, the strategies outlined in this book can help you further develop your confidence.

**3.** *Waiting to do something about your confidence after you lose it.*

Another common mistake athletes make is waiting to act after their confidence is lost. You don't wait to develop a technical problem before you work on technique. Confidence works the same way. Prevention and continued work are key in developing a consistently high level of confidence.

**4.** *Having a wait and see approach to confidence.*

Don't leave confidence to chance. I often ask athletes what comes first, confidence or an event/action that determines their confidence level. Too often, many have a wait and see approach. If they feel good in warmups, then they are confident.  Or they wait and see how the first few minutes go before deciding if they are confident or not. Confidence precedes performance; it comes before an event. Consistent confidence requires us to be proactive, so that you are sure to start with a full tank of confidence rather than waiting to see how you feel.

5. *"My coach took away my confidence."*

Coach can stand for anyone: your parents, friends, significant others, opponents, etc. This is a frequent complaint I hear from athletes that are on the confidence roller-coaster.

Eleanor Roosevelt hit it on the head when she said, *"No one can make you feel inferior without your consent."* If someone takes your confidence away from you, you are making the choice to allow them to do so. While it takes work to develop the habits and skills not to let this happen, no one can take away your confidence without your consent. Confidence is **your** responsibility.

6. *Confidence is an emotion.*

Too many times we think of confidence as an emotion, "I feel confident today" or "I don't feel confident today" and we give into our emotional state. If we give our emotions the power to determine if we are confident or not, then we are held at the mercy of our emotions. Consistent confidence is an action; it's about doing. Like Nike says, "Just do it." Learn to take action instead of just going along with your emotions.

## 7. *Confidence is easily affected by a bad performance.*

Real confidence does not easily fluctuate after a bad play or bad performance. It should not be based on one event. Think of the years you have put into your sport. One bad day should not destroy all the time you have spent developing your craft. If you have a bad outing, the thought should be that it was a bad day, not that you are bad. When you learn to not let one bad performance rob you of your confidence, you start to get off the confidence roller-coaster more quickly.

\*\*\*

If any of the above apply to you, I am here to tell you that it is a choice you have made, even if unknowingly. Maybe until now, you didn't realize it was a choice. However, through your thoughts and actions you alone determine your confidence. My goal is to teach you how to make confidence a daily decision, to start every day with a full tank of confidence just as you would start a trip with a full tank of gas.

When you work at confidence as any other skill, and are proactive and take responsibility for it, you will be more consistent in your performance and have a steady supply of confidence regardless of the circumstance.

Start working on the 4 steps presented in this book daily, and you will learn how to build and maintain a steady supply of confidence. Let's get to doing, and start releasing the emergency brakes.

*"When you have confidence, you can have a lot of fun. And when you have fun, you can do amazing things."*
*—Joe Namath*

# 1

# CONFIDENCE IS TALKING THE TALK

*Every time you speak, you are either increasing or decreasing confidence.*

**Talking the Talk** is simply your self-talk, which is the first step to confidence. Anytime you think about something, you are "talking to yourself." Your self-talk (thoughts) directly impacts the other 3 steps to confidence. Before taking the next steps, you need to first make sure your self-talk lays a strong foundation. How you talk to yourself is a determining factor of your confidence level. What you say to yourself affects what you think and how you feel. If your self- talk is positive, your thoughts and feelings will also be positive. It is almost impossible to think and feel negatively when you're talking positively to yourself.

It is unrealistic to think that all self-talk has to be positive, but if your inner thoughts are not positive, they should at least be productive. Studies show that we have around 50,000 thoughts a day. Most of us do not even realize how much time we spend talking to ourselves. For the majority of people, 90% of those are unproductive thoughts. That is a lot of unproductive self-talk out there! What would happen if we cut that in half? We would be on our way to releasing our confidence emergency brake.

Talking the talk plants the seeds for how you feel which directly correlates to your confidence. Our lives generally move in the direction of our most dominant thoughts. Therefore, the more you engage your mind on productive, positive, and successful thoughts, the more confident you will become.

---

**Our Lives Generally Move in the Direction of Our Most Dominant Thoughts**

---

Think about what you say to yourself after a mistake? Is it positive and/or productive or is it negative and/or unproductive?

Your body will often follow the strongest impression in your mind. If I say, "don't think about the pink elephant in the room," most likely your mind thinks of a pink elephant. If you walk up to the plate thinking "Don't strike out, don't strike out," you're probably going to strike out!  Branch Rickey, a member of the St. Louis Cardinals Hall of Fame once said that, *"A full mind is an empty a bat."* However, I think "*a **negative** mind is an empty at* *bat"* is more appropriate.

Instead of saying, "Don't strikeout." say something along the lines of, "I am going to make good contact with the ball." What you say to yourself influences your body, therefore your actions. Start being proactive by choosing the thoughts you want to give power to. We cannot always control a thought from entering our minds, but we can control the energy we give that thought.

By talking the talk, you are also being your own best ally. When you don't talk the talk, you are then playing against your opponent *and* yourself. As the famous surfer, Laird Hamilton said, *"Make sure your own worst enemy is not living between your own two ears."*

Below are some tips for using **Talking the Talk.** They might not all work for you but find one or two that will help you become more positive and/or productive with your self-talk.

### 1.  Rubber Band Pop

When I was in high school, I had a short fuse with myself when it came to making mistakes or losing. Luckily, I had a coach that had just the cure for it. He handed me a rubber band and told me to wear it on my wrist. Every time I got frustrated or down on myself, I was to pop the rubber band. After numerous pops, it quickly became a reminder to me to have positive or productive thoughts. When working with athletes this is one of the first techniques I give them.

**EXERCISE:** For the first week, wear a rubber band and pop yourself for every negative or unproductive thought. Most people are amazed at the amount of unproductive thoughts they have. In week 2, pop yourself but then change the dialogue. Replace the unproductive thought with a productive one.

## 2.   "I am..." Statements

This is also referred to as affirmations, which are repeated positive statements designed to bring about a desired result. The idea is that, by saying something over and over, you will actually start to believe it.

A Latin proverb states, *"Repetitio est mater studiorum"* which means, *repetition is the mother of all learning.* The more we repeat a thought, or action, the more familiar and comfortable we become with it because we are learning through repetition. Repetition triggers our subconscious mind into positive action.

> *"It's the repetition of affirmations that leads to belief. And once that belief becomes a deep conviction, things begin to happen."*
> *-Muhammad Ali*

Our brain often believes what we tell it. As a result, many of us have developed self-beliefs that do not help us. On a daily basis we get into habits of saying negative statements about ourselves that act like self-fulfilling prophesies.

Think of an elephant at a circus. All the other animals are placed in cages. The elephant, the largest and strongest animal, is only held in place by a single chain around one leg. What prevents this creature from breaking free? Nothing but the chains in its mind. You see, when an elephant is a baby and not nearly as strong, it physically cannot break free from the chain. After many attempts, it slowly believes it isn't strong enough to break the chain. The elephant becomes conditioned to this limiting belief.

We are often like elephants in a circus. We cling to limiting beliefs because we've been criticized or told something negative by someone else (or ourselves), and we hang onto that chain. Or, we haven't had the success we desire, so we have conditioned ourselves to believe we can't do something.

However, just as our negative proclamations become self-fulfilling prophesies, the opposite can be true as well. "I am…" statements help us break these mental chains and increase our chances of more favorable results.

*** 

In my 30s, I started running competitively. I had always despised running up hills. However, it finally dawned on me during a 10k in Asheville, NC, as I was running up a lot of hills, that I needed to apply my own teaching. As I approached each hill, I started telling myself, "I am a hill runner. I am a hill runner...." I continued saying this and before I knew it, I was on the downhill side. Running up hills became easier.

Our brains cannot have 2 separate thoughts at the exact same time. By telling myself I was a hill runner, I prevented negative thoughts from draining my energy and confidence. It is not that I was bad at running hills, it was my self-talk that needed to change. I started applying positive self-talk to all my hill runs and before I knew it I was seeking them out on training runs and looked forward to them during races. What had once been a weakness became a strength just by changing my internal dialogue.

*** 

I once worked with a collegiate softball catcher. She reached out to me after her batting average fell below 100. We tried several strategies before applying the "I am..." statement. She chose to say,

"I am the greatest hitter out here" and would repeat this throughout practices, before games, while on deck, and in the batter's box. She credits the change in her self-talk to improving her batting average by almost 100 points.

\*\*\*

"I am..." statements should be strong and positive. They should focus on what you want instead of what you don't want and should never focus on failure. For example, "I am calm" is stronger than "I am not stressed" or "I will get a hit" is more effective than "I will not strike out." Avoid such words as "maybe," "not," "won't", etc.

**EXERCISE**: List 2-3 things you are not very confident about in your sport. This can range from physical, technical, leadership, tactical, to mental skills. Once you have listed these, create an "I am" statement for each skill. For example, if you aren't as confident with dribbling with your left hand in basketball say, "I am strong with my left." Or if you struggle with late game situations, "I am great when the game is on the line."

- Say your "I am..." statements throughout the day, and especially when practicing or competing.
- Make sure they are in your own words.

- Write them down and place them where you will see them frequently.

## 3.  Vocabulary

Simply changing your vocabulary slightly can make significant improvements in your confidence. Here are some small but powerful words to incorporate into your vocabulary.

**a.  "Yet"**
Too often we start to believe things that haven't happened. For example, "I haven't hit a first serve in," or "we have never beat that team." Placing a **"yet"** at the end of such phrases sends a message to your brain that there is still hope, still a chance.  "I haven't hit my first serve in **yet"** or "we haven't beat that team **yet**".

**b.  "Get to" vs "Have to"**
Often, we get into the habit of saying we "have to" do something, which leads us to negative thoughts. Work on catching yourself saying "have to" and replace with "**get to.**"  For example, "We **get to** do conditioning" versus "we have to do conditioning."  Conditioning may not be fun for you, but if you approach it with a **"get to"** mentality and understand its importance, you will be more productive. The same with

practice. How many times have you said, "I have to go to practice" instead of "I **get to** go to practice?" How confident would you be without conditioning? Without going to practice? Start looking for ways to say you **"get to"** vs "have to" do something.

c. **"I will/I believe/I can…"**
Too many of us are "hopers" (we just hope things will happen). We hope we will make this shot. We hope we will be confident. We hope we will win. Replace hope with **"I will,"** **"I believe I can,"** or **"I know."** A small change in the strength of your words can give your confidence a huge boost.

d. **"But"**
Eliminate the word "but." "But" is nothing more than an excuse. "We would have won but…" "You did this well but…." When someone else says that to us, all we remember is what comes after the "but" or we instantly think it is an "excuse." Your challenge is to eliminate statements that use the word "but."

e. **"This Is Good"**
This phrase has become my motto in my own life. I have learned that "nothing is good or bad until we decide it is." The power is in learning to focus on what is good in a

situation. This is best illustrated in one of my favorite stories:

*A story is told of an African king who had a close friend with whom he grew up. The friend had a habit of looking at every situation that occurred in his life (positive or negative) and remarking, "This is good!" Because of this, the king took his friend with him wherever he went.*

*One day the king and his friend were out on a hunting expedition. As they went along the friend would load and prepare the guns for the king. The friend had apparently done something wrong in preparing one of the guns, for after taking the gun from his friend, the king fired it and his thumb was blown off. Examining the situation, the friend remarked as usual, "This is good!" to which the king replied, "No, this is NOT good!" and angrily sent his friend to jail.*

*About a year later, the king was with his hunting party when they were captured by a band of cannibals. The cannibals began to kill and eat the hunting party one by one.*

*However, when the cannibals got to the king they realized he was missing a thumb. Being superstitious, they never ate anyone who was missing a body part and so, untying the king, they sent him on his way.*

*The king rushed to the jail where his friend was imprisoned and exclaimed, "You saved my life! Thank you, thank you." To which his friend replied, "This is good!"*

*"Yes, this is good for me, but I am sorry for sending you to jail" the king responded. "No," his friend replied, "This is good!"*

*"What do you mean?" asked the king. "How is it good that I sent you to jail for a year?"*

*"If I had NOT been in jail, I would have been with you and been eaten by the cannibals."* (Author unknown)

\*\*\*

Although a bit dramatic, this story illustrates the point that regardless of what happens in life, we have the opportunity to choose our perspective. How we think about a situation internally, our "self-talk", is the starting point for all future action. Working towards a positive outcome in a negative situation begins with positively shaping our self-talk. During moments of adversity, learn to find the positive.

**EXERCISE:** Make a list of things that could go wrong and then list what is good in each situation. Some examples include: being injured, not starting, not playing the position you want, losing, bad calls, etc. Now be proactive and list ways that when/if these situations occur how you would overcome them. For example, you currently aren't playing the position you prefer. Your "this is good" response might be *"this is good because it will make me a more versatile player who can contribute to the team in a variety of ways"*.

> **Nothing is Good nor Bad**
> **Until We Decide It is**

## 4.  Focus on What You Did Right

Instead of pinpointing all the things you did wrong, find what you did well and build on it. I am a recreational golfer. The one thing I love about the game is that I remember the 1 or 2 shots I hit really well, not the 80-90 bad ones! Granted, this is easier since golf is not my main sport. However, I realized that I should take more of the same approach to my main sports of tennis and basketball. Now, I use the same thought process with the athletes I work with.

I'm not saying solely focus only on what you did right but if you focus on the positives from each practice/game and keep building on them you will be amazed at the results. Find the good you are doing and build on it, don't dwell on the negatives (learn from them and move on).

Train your brain to focus on finding the positive and productive actions in your game. The more you focus on these positive/productive things, your brain will adapt to this becoming the norm. We can get overwhelmed and lose confidence when our brains instantly go to what we did wrong. For example, you may have made 6 assists, but you missed the last shot. If you focus on the last shot, you lose what you did well, which takes some of your confidence out of your tank. When you focus on what you did well, you are fueling your confidence level.

**EXERCISE:** After every practice and competition, list 5 specific things that you did well or that went well for you. Date the entry and keep the list in the same notebook or on the same app on your phone. When you need a boost to your confidence tank, you can look back to remind yourself what was positive or productive.

### 5. Focus on Past Successes

This is similar to the above technique, but it highlights more of your past. What happens when you recall past successes? When I ask this to athletes, common answers include: "my confidence increased", "I felt proud," "my body language instantly improved," "it made me feel good about myself," "it made me happy," etc.

Close your eyes for 30-60 seconds and relive a past performance in as much detail as possible. How did it make you feel? If you felt any of the above feelings, use the following exercise to help you build and maintain confidence.

**EXERCISE:** Create an ongoing list of past successes in your sport. Throughout the week, brainstorm as many of your past successes as possible and list in a journal. Continue to add successes as they happen. When you need a jolt of confidence, read through your journal and remember what you have accomplished.

## 6.  Cue Word

A cue word is a word that evokes confidence or reminds our brains to focus on something specific. For example, in tennis a cue word might be something as simple as saying, "footwork", "ball," etc. These reminders, over time, become internalized so that we never think about the placement of our feet or the ball. It becomes automatic and programmed into our neuro-muscular response.

When I played college basketball, I would always say, "money" every time I shot the ball. The word "money" was my cue word and when I said it, it evoked thoughts that my shot was on the money. Several basketball players I have worked with have used, "net" or "swish." There is no right or wrong with a cue word. A tennis player I worked with would say, "ball, ball." This kept his mind focused on the ball and his mind engaged at the same time. The idea is to have your mind focused on this word so that unproductive thoughts don't enter your mind.

**EXERCISE:** Create your own cue word that you will say to yourself when getting ready to shoot, hit, etc. Say it as you perform specific skills in your sport, such as shooting a basketball in the example above.

### 7. Be Your Own Best Friend

Most of us tend to be harder on ourselves than we are on others. A great technique when something happens to you is to think about how you would respond to your best friend and then respond that way to yourself.

**EXERCISE:** Do you have a best friend as a teammate or that plays the same sport? If so, most likely you speak encouraging words to them. For the next week, make a conscious effort to talk encouragingly to yourself as you would your best friend.

## 8. Be Solution Focused vs Problem Focused

Often, we dwell on the problems instead of using our energy to find solutions. Focusing on problems has an indirect effect on our confidence. When we focus on solutions, we are more productive. This doesn't mean we ignore problems, rather, we see problems as an opportunity to make things better. Being solution focused allows us to be less likely to react emotionally to events. The more we train our brains to focus on what we can do about something, the more power we give ourselves, therefore increasing our confidence. Everything that happens can be an opportunity or a threat. It's up to our thinking to determine which it will be.

**EXERCISE**: For 2 weeks, every time you start to dwell on a problem, immediately shift your focus to solutions. Find at least 2 ideas to help with a solution for every problem.

\*\*\*

Work on developing one of these skills and start to "own" it. By that, I mean making it a strength, a skill you can depend on that increases your chances of success. Once you own one of these skills, work on developing another one for your mental toolbox. Slight changes in your self-talk will make significant changes to your confidence levels. Often, the only difference between your best performance and your worst performance is your self-talk. Remember that your brain is hearing what you say! Get to talking!

> *" Self-talk is the most powerful form of communication because it either empowers you or defeats you."*
> *-Unknown*

# Coaches Corner

- Catch your athletes doing things right more often than wrong. A 5-1 ratio is important for any relationship. That means for every 1 criticism you give, find 5 things positive or productive.

- All comments should be genuine.

- Be specific regarding the positive reinforcement.

- Actively challenge your players - know who you can challenge and do so.

- Ask them to rephrase when you hear non-productive self-talk.

- Ask your players to find the "this is good" during times of adversity.

- Encourage your players to have cue words.

- Encourage your players to implement the changes in vocabulary presented in this chapter.

# 2

# CONFIDENCE IS WALKING THE WALK

*Confident Athletes Act, Feel, and Look Confident*

**Walking the Walk** relates to your body language and is an essential part of confidence. Body language plays a major role in projecting how we feel about ourselves. One consistent trait I have observed in my work, is that successful athletes carry themselves a certain way; they move and walk with confidence.

Your body language strongly affects your thoughts. How you carry yourself sends messages to your brain, thereby influencing your self-talk. Your *thoughts* control how you *feel*. How you *feel* drives how you *behave*. *Behaviors* drive results.

> **Body Language affects Your Thoughts**
> **Thoughts *drive* Feelings**
> **Feelings *drive* Behavior**
> **Behavior *drives* Results**

If your shoulders are slouched, your head down and your walk is slow, your thoughts and feelings will most likely be negative. If your head is up and you have a brisk walk to your step, there's a greater likelihood your thoughts and feelings will be positive. Walking the walk involves moving with your head held high, chin up, eyes forward, shoulders back, arms swinging, and a bounce in your step. You look and move like a winner. On the flip side, someone not walking the walk would have their head, eyes, and shoulders down, feet slow and dragging, and no energy in their step. They look and move like a loser.

If you don't believe it, try it. Walk the walk (carry yourself with a strong body language) while saying negative things about yourself. More than likely, you will find it is difficult to do because your thoughts are inconsistent with the signals your body is sending you. Then, try not walking the walk (negative body language as you walk) and say positive things about yourself. Again, it is difficult because your thoughts conflict with what your body is doing.

For increased confidence, act the way you want to feel. If you don't feel confident, then change your body language. Whether you feel confident or not, if you carry yourself as though you are, you can fake it until you make it. **Body language doesn't talk. It SCREAMS!**

Here are some simple exercises to try and help you release your confidence emergency brake. Some of the exercises may seem too simple to make a difference, but again, the slightest changes can make big differences.

After all, a slight change in technique is worth it if it improves your hitting or shooting, isn't it?

Doing something one time does not develop a habit. The first step is to become aware of your body language. Once you are aware, then you can make the necessary changes. New habits are developed by consistently working on making these improvements. The following exercises will help you become more aware and intentional in improving your "**Walk the Walk"**, which will increase your confidence.

### 1. Walk Faster

Think about what a confident person looks like while they are walking. Generally, they are the ones a step ahead of everyone else. One of the surest ways to tell how a person feels about herself is to examine her walk. Is it slow? tired? painful? Or is it energetic and purposeful? People with confidence tend to walk quicker and more upright. Even if you aren't in a hurry, you can increase your self-confidence by putting some pep in your step. Walking faster will make you look and feel more confident.

**EXERCISE:** Throughout the day, look for every opportunity to walk faster. Whether it's to class, from the car to the grocery store, from the locker room to the court, etc. find as many opportunities as possible to walk faster.

## 2.    Good Posture

Just as the pace someone walks sends a message, the way someone holds themselves paints a clear picture about their confidence. If you sit up straight, you will feel more energetic and in control. People with slumped shoulders and lethargic movements are sending out a message to others, and more importantly to themselves, that they aren't very confident. Slumped posture indicates that either you are not interested or that you don't feel like you belong. Having good posture will instantly give you a jolt of confidence. Stand up straight, keep your head up and make eye contact, and you will feel more energetic and in control.

There have been several studies on the scientific evidence behind power posing. Some have concluded that standing or sitting a certain way, for two minutes, raises testosterone levels and lowers the stress hormone, cortisol. Why is this important? Because these hormones affect the way you perform and interact. There is significant evidence and a high correlation that these hormonal changes will have a strong influence on your success. When released, these hormones are telling your brain to be confident.

## A.  Superman/Wonder Woman Pose

This idea works with any pose that evokes strength. The vision of Superman or Wonder Woman standing broad, with hands on waist, elbows out, chest out, and chin and head up, creates the perfect picture of a strong, powerful, and confident pose.

**EXERCISE**: Every morning and prior to practices and games, stand for 2-3 minutes in a power pose. For an additional boost, add some confident self-talk while standing.

## B.  Ideal Body Language

Recall some of your more confident moments. Remember what your body language looked like and what it felt like.

**EXERCISE:** During practice and competitions imitate your ideal body language. When you make a mistake immediately return your body to this ideal state.

## 3.  Other Body Awareness Exercises:

### A.  Puppet on a String

Picture the old timey wooden puppets on strings. To make these puppets move or express themselves, you had to pull on their strings.

**EXERCISE:** When you recognize that you are slumped or not in ideal body language, imagine a string running through the top of your head and pulling you upright. Pull yourself up just as if you were a puppet.

**B.  Look to the Sky**
Another way to break negative body language is to look upward and hold your gaze for a few seconds. This simple action can break your negative thoughts.

**EXERCISE**: For one week, when you recognize that your body language is poor, break the negative thoughts by looking up.

**4.  Control Your Face**

Your facial expressions often convey what you are feeling. Learn to control your facial expressions and you will slowly take control over the story your face conveys. In the process, you will slowly take over what you are feeling as well. The belief is that if one smiles long enough, he or she will eventually feel good about themselves. People in sales are often trained to do this to increase their sales.

**EXERCISE:** When you are upset during practice or an event, get into the habit of smiling. Work on avoiding expressions of negativity and irritability.

### 5.   Walk the Walk Ritual

Take a 3-5 minute walk and keep your focus on displaying strong body language. Doing this in the morning can set the tone for the day, especially if you implement some positive self-talk and use your ideal body image from the previous exercises.

**EXERCISE:**  Take a 3-5 minute walk, focusing on strong body language every day for 2 weeks.  In addition, take this walk prior to a competition to get your confidence level as high as you can.

*** 

While not all of these exercises will work for every individual, the key is to find the ones that will work for you. How we walk and carry ourselves influences our confidence a great deal. Remember that *body language* affects your *thoughts,* which create your *feelings.*  Your *feelings* drive your *behaviors and your behaviors* strongly impact your results.  Get to walking!

*ABC= Always Behave Confidently!*

# Coaches Corner

- Pete Carroll, coach of the Seattle Seahawks believes that during competition, "Coaches should either be a poker player or a cheerleader." Most athletes know when they have messed up. Keep a poker face and try not to show negative emotions on your face and with your body language.
*This isn't to say never get on them, but do so in a productive manner and when time allows you to effectively coach (which usually isn't in the middle of a play).*

- Your own body language influences that of your athletes therefore, act accordingly.

- Touch is important because it connects people. Give high fives, fist bumps, a hug when needed, pat on back, etc. This body language connection can be a confidence boost.

- Emphasis the importance of good body language to your athletes. Challenge them to correct their body language when needed.

- If available show game film of your athletes' body language.  Often, they are not aware of what they look like.

# 3
# TALKING the TALK & WALKING the WALK

*"If you can't control your emotions,*
*then your emotions will control you."*
*-Anurag Prakash Ray*

Emotions can be good or bad for our confidence. I was once told an analogy about emotions and fire. When emotions are blazing out of control, they are like a wildfire burning and destroying everything in its path. However, when emotions are under control, they are like a fire in a fireplace keeping you warm. When we take charge of our emotions, our confidence will soar under control, like the fire in the fireplace.

Consistent confidence involves both your mind and body. Recall in the last chapter that our body language affects our thoughts, which drives our emotions and ultimately, our results. Therefore, if we want to control our emotions, the key is to talk the talk and walk the walk. Applied together, these two actions can create almost any mood or emotion you desire.

Let me ask you a question to demonstrate this. Could you cry for $1000? Most people could. Occasionally, when I ask that question in team sessions, there is a person or two that actually produces tears.

How would you do it? Most people would think about something sad and change their posture. Their posture would become weak, shoulders would slump, and they may even get in a fetal position with a frown or pout on their faces.

Now, if you were having a bad day and I said I'd give you $1000 to start smiling and acting happy, how would you do it? This is a little bit easier, but the same process occurs. You would think of something that made you happy, put a smile on your face even if it was forced at first, and your body language would be relaxed.

In both instances, it is the self-talk and body language that allows the mood to change. Too often, we go with the emotion we are feeling instead of using our talk and our walk to change to a more productive, successful mood. Using this logic, if you want to be confident, then talk yourself into it by thinking of something that makes you confident, and by walking yourself into it with strong body language. If you do not easily feel confident, fake it until you make it- *talk the talk and walk the walk.*

**EXERCISE:** Practice being able to control your moods by seeing how long it takes you to portray the following emotions by talking the talk and walking the walk.

*Happy    *Silly    *Funny    *Serious    *Confident
*Mad      *Sad      *Grateful  *Bossy      *Loose

Challenge yourself even further by adding other emotions to this list.

***

I do a lot of traveling in my business and I often use the travel time to plan sessions, brainstorm new ideas, and try out techniques.  A few years ago, I was on a 5 ½ hour drive and I decided to do a similar exercise as the one I just mentioned. I was driving down the road (NOTE: *do not follow my lead and do while driving!*), and for a few minutes I created a serious mood, then I changed it to ecstatic, then to anger and so on. I was completely in the moment of the current emotion. At some point, I could feel someone staring at me. I looked out my window and in the car in the left lane was an elderly lady with a look of shock and concern. I waved politely but didn't think much about it. Seeing that I needed gas, I took the next exit and pulled into a gas station. The elderly lady and her husband pulled in beside me. She rolled down her window and asked in a rather concerned voice, "Miss are you ok? You sure looked crazy while you were driving, and we wanted to make sure you were ok." Embarrassment quickly became the emotion I was feeling. How could I explain that I was trying out a technique for work? I laughed to myself thinking the sight I must have been, assured her that I was fine, and thanked her for asking.

The reason for sharing this story, is that obviously the technique worked. I was so engrossed in my emotions by talking the talk and walking the walk that I actually was showing them in my body language. I also share this story to demonstrate that I use the techniques I give my athletes and coaches.

***

Connecting with your teammates through your talk and walk, helps build confidence as well. UC Berkeley did a study that showed teams that talk and touch the most usually win the most. I call this T-N-T (Talk -n- Touch). When you are talking the talk and walking the walk with your teammates, it creates a collective confidence for not only the individual, but also the team. If you are productively talking to your teammates and you are giving strong body language and interaction, you naturally will be more confident. For one, you are focused on something that helps the team instead of something negative about yourself. Also, touch is a powerful weapon! Steve Nash, former 2x NBA MVP was a great example of this. He gave around 240 high fives a game.

**EXERCISE:** Every practice and competition, make it a habit to T-N-T with every teammate. Find a way to encourage, cheer, give constructive criticism, etc. Also look for opportunities to give them high fives, fist bumps, pats on the back, or even picking them up when they are on the ground.

***

We can think our way to a new level of acting, but when we also walk our way to a new level of thinking, it magnifies our confidence. Using our thoughts and body language allows us to take control of our emotions. When we ae in charge of emotions, it's easier to release our confidence emergency brakes. ***Talk the talk and walk the walk and fake it 'til you make it!***

*In Everything You Do, THINK and ACT Like a Winner*

# 4
# CONFIDENCE IS SEEING IT TO BE IT

*"The secret of achievement is to hold a picture of the success outcome in mind"  -Henry David Thoreau*

**See it Be it** - Confidence comes from seeing what you want (seeing is believing). You need to see what you want to be. This means seeing a picture in your mind of how you want things to go or how you want to be. By creating a clear image in your head of what you want to happen, you are planting seeds of confidence. This step is stronger than self-talk because it goes a step further by adding a vision to your self-talk; it creates a picture of your thoughts.

Visualization stimulates the same areas in the brain that are used when you are actually doing the same action. Your brain doesn't know the difference between actually doing something or visualizing it in detail.

If you see yourself as an average athlete or picture yourself performing mediocre before or during a training session or competition, the chances increase that mediocrity will be your reality. On the flipside, if you imagine yourself performing as you desire and create pictures in your mind of yourself as confident and prepared, chances increase that you will be more successful. Visualizing how you want to look and perform plants the seeds for success and gives you an extra edge.

Not only should you see success, but you should picture adversity as well. Rarely does everything go as you want it to. Sports are filled with adversity. By picturing adversity happening and seeing yourself overcoming it, you are preparing yourself for when adversity actually does occur. This naturally increases your confidence. You feel ready for anything. For steady confidence, we need to see success in any circumstance.

In his book, *For the Love of the Game: My Story*, Michael Jordan admits that his biggest strength wasn't his height or physical skill. It was his ability to visualize.

A study on visualization was done at Ohio University with 3 control groups shooting free throws. Each group's free throw shooting percentage was measured at the beginning of the study. During the study, group 1 was only allowed to practice free throws for an hour a day. Group 2 spent half of this time practicing and the other half visualizing. Group 3 used the entire time only visualizing shooting free throws. At the end of the study, guess which group showed the most improvement? If you guessed Group 2, you are right.

**Note:** *While visualizing is important, do not use it as an excuse to not practice. A combination of both is what will likely give you the best results.*

***

**3 Ways to Help You See It So You Can Be It**

**1. See Yourself as a Winner**

Condition your brain for success, by seeing how you want the day, practice, and/or the competition to go. View yourself performing with confidence- actually picture what your confident self looks like. In this mental image, focus on your strengths which will make you successful. In as much detail as possible, picture how you want things to go, and see yourself performing your personal best.

***

The following story is about a high school softball team I worked with. It is a great example of the power of visualization, seeing yourself as a winner and planting the seeds every day.

From day one, the team had the goal of winning a state championship, which was not an impossible task as they were a solid team but would still face plenty of challenges and intense competition. The first session I had with them, I discussed the importance of visualization and gave them homework. I told them if they were serious about winning the state title, then they could and would do these things every night:

- Visualize having the game winning at bat.
- Visualize making the game winning defensive play.
- Visualize how good it would feel when that last out was recorded and you were celebrating with your teammates.

To make a long story short, they made it to the state championship. Along the way, they had several miraculous comebacks. During an elimination game, they were down by 7 in the bottom of the 7th with 2 outs and rallied for the win. The confidence they had to overcome this deficit was aided by visualization. They had visualized being winners for so long there was no doubt in anyone's mind they would triumph.

In the third and final game of the state championship, one of the players got a base hit in the top of the 1st inning that later led to a run. In between innings, this player came to me and said, "I know that it is only the 1st inning and there will probably be more base hits and runs, but that was exactly what I have been seeing every night." Little did any of us know that was the only hit and only run that this explosive offensive team would produce all game. Every inning, the other team kept the pressure on by getting runners to second or third base, yet never getting a run across. In the bottom of the 7th still up 1-0 with 2 outs, everyone sensed and felt a state championship was ours. Then the wheels fell off. An easy hit back to the pitcher resulted in an error, and the next batter hit the ball to second where another miscue took place. Now the opponent's best hitter was at the plate with 2 out and 2 runners on, and a base hit would likely tie or win the game. She proceeded to launch one to right field. It seemed like it would be a routine catch for the sure-handed right fielder until she tripped a little. For a second, everyone's hearts dropped; this was how it was going to end. Then in the next second, she was able to gather herself and reach up and snag the ball. Mayhem erupted. Later on that evening, she texted me and said, the only reason she was able to maintain her cool and make the catch was because she had pictured every day, since day one, that she was going to make the game winning catch. By seeing it every day, it gave her the confidence to overcome a misstep.

I wish I could say visualization works this well every time, but this was a fairy tale ending. However, this fairy tale happened because the players on this team consistently visualized being winners. You too, can use visualization to put yourself in position for success when your opportunity arises.

***

As a college tennis coach, I saw a similar example of the power of seeing yourself as a winner. Our university had just reclassified from DII to DI. We were joining an extremely challenging mid-major conference in tennis. In the preseason rankings, we were predicted to finish last. None of us really knew what to expect, but I was sitting with my #1 player at a volleyball match and I shared a dream from the night before. I said, "You know Anna, I dreamed that we won the conference last night." She looked at me big eyed and asked, "Yeah?" I said, "I think we can if we believe it, and if we see it every day." Not much was said after that. However, the next day at practice, Anna told the rest of the team to start seeing us winning every day. She would finish every practice reminding them to imagine it that night. That season was a whirlwind. One by one, we knocked off conference opponents to set up a showdown for the conference title between the reigning champions and us.

It was a dramatic match. Anna was losing to the #1 girl in the conference who was highly ranked nationally. In addition, we were losing at most positions. We all kept telling each other to believe and remember what we had seen all year. Not only did Anna come back and win in the third set, but our 5th and 6th singles, after dropping the first set, both came back and won in the third. After the exuberance and celebration calmed down, I talked to several of our players. Each one in their own words told me that they never doubted because they had planted success in their heads every day, all season. When the match was on the line, they had confidence because they had virtually been there every day of the season. That's powerful, but visualization is a powerful tool if you use it consistently.

***

Michael Jordan, arguably the greatest to ever play basketball, daily visualized making the game winning shot, which he did numerous times. Carli Lloyd imagined her goals before every match. During the 2015 World Cup, she visualized herself scoring four goals in the championship. Lloyd didn't quite make her goal of four, but she did make a hat trick (3 goals) which no one else had ever done on that stage.

**EXERCISE:** Every morning find a comfortable place to sit or lie. Then take a few deep breaths and for 2-3 minutes, see in vivid detail how you want the day, practice, and/or the competition, etc. to go. Imagine your ideal body language. See yourself performing at a high level, and how that will make you feel. Throughout the day, picture the confident, successful you.

**EXERCISE:** Everyday, visualize 5 minutes scoring the winning goal, making the winning save, etc. Then from your past successes create your own highlight reel.

2. **Get in Extra Reps**

See yourself running specific plays, making plays, making shots, etc. See the technical and tactical aspects of your sport in detail. Using visualization to get in extra reps and practice, creates neural patterns in your brain. These patterns engrave the performance on your brain cells and it creates muscle memory (just as if you were physically practicing). This can be extremely helpful when injured, if you are behind tactically or technically, during recovery times, or when other events don't allow for normal practices.

\*\*\*

One of my favorite stories of using visualization for getting extra reps, is the story of Laura Wilkinson, an Olympic diver for the United States. Wilkinson had just qualified for the 2000 Olympics, when she broke her foot. With just six months left before the start of the Games, she was unable to train. Most would have felt hopeless, that their dreams of competing in the Olympics, much less win a gold medal, were gone.

Wilkinson, however stayed confident and focused on what she could still do, which was train mentally. She spent hours each day visualizing every turn, flip, etc. of each dive. She would see herself walking up to the diving board preparing for her dives, and then she would see herself performing perfectly. She even imagined herself climbing out of the pool. She saw every detail of her performance numerous times a day.

Many would say what happened is just short of a miracle. Despite this setback and despite being a heavy underdog to the Chinese, Wilkinson performed to near perfection to win the gold. She was more prepared than she had ever been. By using visualization, she knew how she would perform and when she stepped up on the platform it felt as if she had been there hundreds of times before.

***

A collegiate volleyball player I was working with had an ongoing injury. The trainers and coaches tried to manage her ability to play by limiting her practice time. She naturally felt less confident. I asked her to start practicing in her mind each day. During practices, when she wasn't participating, her goal was to mentally put herself in place of a teammate playing the same position and imagine it was her out there on the floor. At night, she was to get reps in her head by seeing herself hitting from numerous positions, as well as seeing herself blocking various balls. She ended up having an all-conference season despite being limited at practice. She credits her ability to have a successful year by her consistent application of getting extra reps through visualization.

**EXERCISE:** Prior to practice and competition, see yourself taking shots (swings, etc.) from various positions on the court, field, or course. For example, golfers should see themselves taking shots from all over the golf course, batters should see themselves in different hitting situations and hitting different pitches with different counts. For sports that have a defensive component, spend time visualizing making the catch to end the inning, making the sliding tackle that saves a goal, etc.

**EXERCISE:** In situations where you start the action (i.e. foul shot in basketball, all golf shots, set pieces in soccer, pitching in softball and baseball, serves in sports such as tennis and volleyball), see what you want to happen right before the play starts or resumes. Plant the seed for how you want that shot, pitch, bat, etc. to go.

**EXERCISE:** If you aren't playing due to an injury or being on the bench, make sure visualization is in your mental toolbox. Implementing visualization in this instance, will keep you prepared for when your time comes.

3. **Embrace Adversity**

See bad calls, bad plays, missed shots, etc. and see yourself successfully overcoming them. I often get asked why I want my athletes to see something bad. Bad things happen in every practice and every competition, every day. Therefore, I want you to visualize your response to the adversity so when it happens you are prepared and confident. Practicing in your mind how you will respond to the challenge, will give you confidence.

\*\*\*

The great Michael Phelps relied on visualization to set world records. During the 200m butterfly at the Beijing Olympics in 2008, Phelps dove into the water and right away his goggles started to fill with water. As he touched the wall on the final turn, he could no longer see anything. Instead of panicking, he relied on the numerous times he had mentally practiced that race in his head. Not only did his visualization training allow him to win gold, he also beat his own world record. Asked afterwards how it felt to have that adversity in such an important race, Phelps replied: *"Like I imagined it would."*

*** 

A college soccer team that I was working with really bought into using visualization to overcome adversity. Every night before a match, they would imagine things that could go wrong and see themselves saying "This is Good" and overcoming it. This was put to the test against a rival team. Only 6 minutes into the match, the Keeper received a red card (therefore placing my team a man down for the rest of the game). The backup keeper without any warm-up in her first collegiate match, stepped up and helped this team beat their rival team, while playing a man down. I asked the backup afterward how she felt when she realized she was going in her first college match facing this adversity. She calmly told me that she felt confident because she had been imagining overcoming such adversity every night.

**EXERCISE:** Prior to practice and competition, take 1-2 minutes to imagine various negative/challenging events that could happen (bad call, error on your end, etc.). Then imagine in detail, how you will respond if and when this happens. A contest is never perfect; challenging events happen. By seeing these events and practicing them ahead of time, you will be more prepared and confident when they actually do happen.

***

One of the biggest complaints I hear from athletes I work with, is that they see bad things happening when they try to visualize. My response is that there is a reason they are seeing negative things happening. Normally, 9 out of 10 times the root of the problem lies in their self-talk. Their self-talk, a.k.a. thoughts, have planted the seed of something bad happening. Be intentional, keep replacing the negative thoughts with positive, productive ones, until you develop this as habit.

Another thing I sometimes hear about using visualization is that it doesn't work right away, or all the time. Like any skill, it will take *intentional* practice and repetition to make visualization a habit. So, do not be deterred if at first it doesn't work. Remember, you are developing a new skill, which takes practice.

Seeing things before they happen adds another level of confidence. When we are uncomfortable or not as secure due to lack of practice, inexperience etc., we are likely to be less confident. By mentally rehearsing situations as much as possible, you are creating repetitions in your brain and therefore building confidence. In addition, the more vivid and frequent you see your goals, how you want to be, etc. in your mind, the more likely they become reality. Visualization is a strong step in releasing confidence emergency brakes. After all, seeing is believing. Get to seeing!

*"Visualization is daydreaming with a purpose"*
*- Bo Bennett*

# Coaches Corner

- Visualize what you as a coach want to happen for your athletes and team.

- Visualize your athletes and team overcoming challenges and adversity.

- Plant in your players' minds what you want them to see.

- Encourage your athletes to make visualization a part of their daily routine.

- Conduct a pre-game mental rehearsal with your team to reinforce the game strategy as well as to plant the seeds for success.

# 5
# Confidence is Being Prepared

*"Confidence is preparation. Everything else is*
*beyond your control"*
*-Richard Kline*

**P**reparation is the foundation of confidence. It is difficult to maintain confidence when you know you have cut corners, or not taken care of your body, or slacked in your physical or mental preparation. However, when you put in the time and the work and you know you have done all you can do, you have laid a strong building block for confidence.

### Preparation + Repetitions = Consistency

When you put in the practice hours, preparing your body physically and mentally, consistency occurs. Preparation cannot be a sometimes thing. The most successful athletes prepare very carefully for every competition as well as every practice. They have a set mental and physical routine that they follow daily. They don't leave things to chance, and not just on game day or the day before. Preparation is an **EVERYDAY** thing. The motto for the United States Olympic Committee reads:

> **Not Every Four Years,**
> **It's Every Day**

Know that you did what you could do (DON'T LEAVE ANYTHING TO CHANCE).

Consistent behavior gets consistent performances. Compare your sport to academics. If you consistently prepare by studying, turning assignments in on time, knowing the material, asking questions, staying focused during class and exams, etc. your grades are likely to improve and be better than if you only did some of these things some of the time. The same applies with sports. If you make sure you have all the equipment you need ready to go, you arrive to practice on time, ask questions, know the plays, stay focused through drills, etc. you can't help but get better.

*Consistent performance is the result of consistent behavior. Consistent behavior requires a consistent pattern of thought. It is a **MINDSET.***

Consistency occurs through mental discipline (repeatedly doing the little things irrespective of circumstance or consequence). What are the little things you need to do daily to be prepared? What routines do you need to add? Here are 5 areas of preparation for you to think about.

## The 5 Areas of Preparation

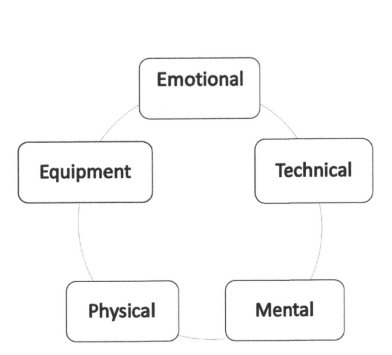

# 1. Emotional

## A. Park Issues

Are you carrying emotional baggage or worries into practices or contests? If so, you are slowly eroding your confidence as well as a chance for success. A good idea is to "park" or temporarily drop your issues before going onto the court or field. Develop a routine that allows you to place all worries aside during practice or competition. The following are 3 examples which my clients have successfully used:

### *Ditch the Demons*
Athletes write their emotional baggage on a piece of paper and ditch it in a specified container. Afterwards, they are free to reclaim the paper and pick the baggage back up.

### *Role Shift Routine*
Athletes create a routine that allows them to start shifting their focus (using self-talk, body language, and visualization) from boyfriend/girlfriend, daughter/son, student, friend, etc. to that of athlete.

### *Rubber band*
The rubber band pop is a great technique to stay emotionally in charge (refer back to the rubber band exercise in Chapter 1: Talk the Talk). When

athletes catch themselves worrying about emotional baggage, they pop the rubber band on their wrist. This serves as a reminder to get back to the task at hand and away from the emotional challenges.

**EXERCISE:** Develop your own routine to at least temporarily drop the emotional baggage while on the playing field. There is no right or wrong way. More importantly, it is finding a routine that will consistently work for you.

## B.  Gratitude

In addition to parking issues not related to the contest, emotional preparation can also take the form of gratitude. By making sure you stay grateful for being able to play the game you love, you are preparing yourself mentally. This can help you take the edge off when you remind yourself it's suppose to be fun. Sometimes we stress and think of the pressure associated with our sport instead of focusing on "getting" the opportunity to play.

Many of us started participating in our sport because we loved it, not to get a college scholarship or to play professionally. Remembering why we play helps us keep our focus more on enjoying the sport instead of adding pressure that we have to perform well to get to the next level.

> *"Somewhere behind the athlete you've become and the hours of practice and the coaches who have pushed you is a little girl who fell in love with the game and never looked back... play for her."*
> — *Mia Hamm*

Additionally, being grateful helps us keep our focus on what's important. When you stop and recall why you started playing your sport, it often helps you relax and therefore able to play better.

**EXERCISE:** On a notecard, list the following: why you started playing your sport and why you still enjoy playing. Read it daily or as needed for a reminder.

**C.  Gratitude Toward Others**

Gratitude also extends to other people. None of us would be here without other people. In the daily grind of life, we sometimes fail to recognize what others have done to help us be where we are. The following true story illustrates how we sometimes fail to recognize others.

*Charles Plumb was a US Navy jet fighter pilot in Vietnam.  During a mission, he was shot down.*

*Plumb ejected and parachuted into enemy hands. After six years in captivity, he survived and was freed.*

*One day while eating at a restaurant, a man came up and said, "You're Plumb! You flew jet fighters in Vietnam from the aircraft carrier Kitty Hawk. You were shot down!*

*"How in the world did you know that?" asked Plumb. "I packed your parachute," the man replied. Charles Plumb in surprise and gratitude had to catch his breath.*

*The man then shook his hand and said, "I guess it worked!" Plumb assured him, "It sure did. If your chute hadn't worked, I wouldn't be here today."*

*That night Plumb could not sleep. He said, "I kept pondering what he might have looked like in a Navy uniform. I wonder how many times I might have seen him and not even said good morning, or how are you or anything, because, you see, I was a fighter pilot and he was just a sailor."*

*Plumb thought a lot about that man who had packed his parachute and the hours he spent at a wooden table at the bottom of the ship carefully packing his and other's chutes. He held in his hands the chute; the fate of someone he did not even know.*

***

In our athletic careers, many people have a hand in packing our parachutes. It is very easy to overlook the work of those that sacrificed for us.

Do we thank the parents, coaches, staff members, and others in our past that believed in us, that gave of themselves, so we could be where we are today?

Who on your team/staff works on your parachute? Thank them today and play for them tonight. When we recognize those that have helped us get where we are today, it strengthens us emotionally.

**EXERCISE:** Dedicate each contest or the season, to someone that has packed your parachute. Send them a text, email or call them and let them know how much influence they have had in where you are today. If they are deceased, play in their memory.

## 2. Technical/Tactical

Do you put everything into practice that you can? Are you intentional with your practice? Too often, athletes go through the motions during practice instead of being fully engaged. The more engaged and focused you are, the better your chance of improving and being prepared at game time. Use your self-talk, body language, and visualization to stay engaged.

Do you do extra skill work on your own? Every team in America practices 2-3 hours a day with a day or 2 off each week. So, what are you doing to set yourself apart?

Additionally, do you know your coaches' game plan for you and your team? When you know what the coach wants from you as well as knowing your role in the plan, you will be much more prepared when the time comes.

**EXERCISE**: Create a goal of putting in a certain number of extra hours each week. If you are unsure where to begin, ask a coach or another expert to give you advice of specific drills you can do. Challenge yourself to reach this goal for 3 weeks.

## 3. Equipment

Having your equipment prepared may not seem like a big deal, but if you find that you forgot to pack something, or your gear is not in good shape it is one more thing to worry about and can affect your confidence.

I learned this lesson the hard way. I swam competitively in Junior High School and my parents would travel with me throughout the south for swim meets. We arrived at a rather important swim meet. I went to change to get ready for warm-ups, only to realize I had forgotten my swimsuit- of all things! Fortunately for me, a teammate was willing to lend me her suit once she finished her race.

Putting on a wet, 2 sizes smaller swimsuit does nothing for your confidence! By not preparing and making sure I had everything I needed, I automatically put myself behind the 8 ball and did not put myself in a position to do the best I could.

During my time as a college tennis coach, I had a prerequisite that my athletes had to have at least 3 recently strung racquets for each match. In addition, they had a checklist of items to include in their bag (from a change of shirt, to snacks, to string, etc.). My belief was that if they had everything, they could possibility need, they would not waste energy thinking and wondering if they forgot something and what they were going to do about it. Planning ahead is preparation, and as small as it seems, it adds to confidence.

**EXERCISE:** Make a checklist for everything you will possibly need for each contest. Below is a checklist of what I would send to my teams prior to every match:

*Example of an Equipment Checklist:*

**What's in your bag?**
- At least one (preferably 2-3) extra, well-strung tennis racket
- Include at least one new can of tennis balls
- Band-Aids and other first aid items you generally need
- Extra t-shirts, socks, etc.
- A towel

- Water bottle, energy drink, etc.
- Energy bars, peanut butter crackers, fruit, etc.
- Visor or hat
- Sunscreen
- Wristbands and headbands
- Extra hair tie for those with long hair
- Pen or pencil and a small notepad or index cards
- Rubber bands
- Your affirmations/cue words, etc. written on note card
- Other:

## 4. Physical

Being physically prepared includes strength, conditioning, and flexibility. Fitness has a huge impact on confidence. If you're out of shape, you will feel insecure, less confident, and less energetic. By working out, you improve your appearance, energize yourself, and increase confidence. Working out not only makes you feel better, but it also creates positive momentum that you can build on. *When you have put in the work, you can't help but be confident.*

I played tennis and basketball in college and I struggled with my confidence. During this time, I put on about 20 additional pounds. I had a teammate that encouraged me to get in shape and start eating better. That summer, I not only dropped the weight but was in the best shape of my life. The newfound confidence in my body quickly transferred onto the court.

Physical preparation also includes proper hydration, eating to fuel your body, getting the proper amount of sleep, resting on your off days, stretching, icing, etc. Your body is your vehicle. It can be the biggest asset or biggest weakness you have. Take care of your body and keep it in proper working condition and your confidence will soar.

**EXERCISE:** Develop a plan to help you achieve a high level of fitness specific for your sport. Look at areas that maybe you are weaker in and make a plan on how to improve those areas. Ask sport coaches, strength and conditioning coaches, trainers, etc. to help you.

## 5. Mental

Mental Preparation is directly related to one's mental strength. *You cannot help but be more confident when you feel prepared.* **The more prepared, the stronger the MIND.** Mental preparation involves the other 3 steps of confidence:  talk the talk, walk the walk, and see it.

Mental preparation means readiness. It means you have prepared your body, your equipment, and your mind, and are ready to execute. Now it's time to warm-up. Do you have a mental warm-up? How would you feel if you were told to just start practicing or playing without dynamic stretching, or getting sport specific reps in? For most of us, we probably wouldn't start out as confidently. The same with the brain. Studies have shown that a mental warm-up prior to practice and contests has a strong correlation to starting 20% faster.

### A. Mental Warm-Up

The goal of a mental warm-up is to start the transition into the role of performer. In a warm-up, you have to plan and prepare for as many situations as possible. Also, this is the time to make sure your tank of confidence is high.

Elite performers are confident because they have developed a consistent series of steps before each performance to help them reach the mental state needed to perform their best. They use a consistent mental warm-up regardless of the opponent or circumstances; regardless if it's a practice, an easy non-conference game, a rival, or a championship game.

Many athletes make the mistake of having have no plan or vary their pre-game approach. **Remember, consistent preparation leads to consistent confidence.** It is important that athletes use a routine that works for them. There is not an ideal routine that works for everyone.

I would suggest starting with music. Create your game day play-list or play that one song over and over that gets you in the right mood to perform at your best. Playing that one song on repeat helps some athletes. I worked with a tennis player, that after listening to the same song over and over, would start singing to himself on the court. When he was singing to himself, we both knew his confidence was at a high. For him, it meant that he was in the flow, not overthinking, and most likely performing at a high level. Others such as Michael Phelps, find it helpful to have a playlist. His go-to music was a playlist that pumped him up so that he was in that right state of mind before diving into the pool.

In addition to music, several suggestions to include in a mental warm-up would consist of: making sure your self-talk and body language is strong, visualizing yourself overcoming possible adversities and seeing yourself having success, as well as making sure your energy level is at its optimal level.

**EXERCISE:** Develop a mental game warm-up. Include the 4 steps of confidence. I would suggest music that gets you in a mood in which you best perform. Then, take long deep breathes to relax yourself. Use self-talk, your body language, and visualization to get your mind and body ready to go. Do your mental warm-up prior to every practice and contest. Remember that consistency is the key.

*Example of a Mental Warm-up:*

- Find a quiet place or put on some ear buds. Listen to a playlist or a song on repeat that creates your ideal mood for game time.
- Take several deep breaths to relax your body.
- Scan your self-talk and body language. If either is weak or unconfident, correct as needed. Make sure you start the competition talking the talk and walking the walk.
- See things that could go wrong and see yourself overcoming them.
- See yourself as a winner and performing at a high level.
- End with a highlight reel of past performances.

### B. Routines During Competition

Routines are important "habits" athletes develop and use during competition to aid in preparation. When you have routines in place, you are able to make better choices and more easily face any challenges that occur. You can't plan for everything, but when the basics are taken care of, you can more easily handle the challenges that occur in sports.

Think of your morning routine. Most of us don't have to think about it in the morning. Your alarm goes off, some of us might hit the snooze while others hit the floor running. Then we each have an unconscious plan we follow which might go something like- go to the bathroom, jump in the shower, brush teeth, fix hair, grab breakfast and make our way to school or work. Think about what happens when your alarm doesn't go off. This throws many off their routine and often their day starts a little more challenging. The same idea applies to routines in sports.  They are used to settle our minds and prepare us for the day.

A mental warm-up mentioned previously, is a type of pre-competition routine. Now, we'll talk about two other routines that can assist you in being prepared during action.

**\*Mistake Routine**

Another way to mentally prepare, is to have a mistake routine. We all are going to make mistakes, but those that are best prepared to handle them are the ones usually most successful. A routine that you do after each mistake, generally will allow you to recover more quickly and move past the mistake. The idea is to do the mistake routine immediately after you make a mistake, which triggers your brain to move forward instead of dwelling on the past mistake.

What I suggest to athletes I work with is to have a physical response combined with a verbal response. For a physical response, you might pop your rubber band (see chapter 2) to snap out of it, take a deep breath and blow your mistake away, a slap on your thigh, brushing your shoulder with your fingertips as if to brush the mistake away, etc.

A verbal response can be anything you say to yourself that will change your focus away from the mistake and toward the task at hand. Some people use words that make them laugh. A high school baseball team I worked with would say "snowflake" when they made mistakes. I never knew the meaning of it, it was an inside joke, but it often worked. Saying the word, would break the negative, unproductive mood they were in.

Other examples might be, "This is good," "next point," "next play," "shake it off," "flush it." Like most of the mental game, the important thing is to choose something that you use consistently and that works for you.

**EXERCISE:** Create your own mistake ritual. Like most techniques I am giving you in this book, there is no right or wrong routine. What's important is that it's a routine you do consistently as well as something that helps you move on after a mistake.

*Tips:*

- You can use visualization to practice your mistake routine. When you see yourself making a mistake, picture yourself doing your mistake routine and moving on toward success. Practice this 5-10 times a day (even if you aren't involved in your sport at that moment).

- Start incorporating your routine in practices and then add to competition.

- It is often beneficial to share your routine with a teammate or coach. When we are in the moment, we often forget to apply such principles. Having someone to serve as a reminder can be helpful.

**\*Pre-Action Routines**

There are times in most sports, where we have a chance to think about what we are doing instead of just reacting (i.e. pitching, shooting a foul shot, hitting a golf shot, serves in service sports, set pieces in soccer, starts in sports such as running events and swimming and diving, etc.). In such cases, the mental aspect of the sport starts before the real action. For example, a golfer's preparation for hitting a shot begins long before the actual swing. Pre-action routines prepare you mentally as well as physically. They ensure you are confident, focused, and ready to perform. Additionally, routines prevent unnecessary negative thoughts from coming into play.

### *Example of a Pre-At Bat Routine for Baseball or Softball:*

**1. Have a Specific Plan**
a.  While on deck take think about the pitches you will most likely see and the game situation.
b.  Know what pitches you are looking for.
c. Start focusing on the pitcher's release point.

**2. Commit to Your Plan**
a.  Be confident with your plan. Do not second guess yourself.
b. When you doubt yourself, you send mixed messages to your body.

**3. Focus on Having a Productive at Bat**
a.  Do not worry about the results of your at bat (you cannot control this).
b.  Focus on the plan only.
c.  Baseball/softball is a game of

managing your mistakes. Most good hitters are thrown out or strike out 7 out of 10 times.

4. **Strong Body Language, Positive Thoughts & Images**
   a. This enables you to have control over your mind.
   b. See yourself hitting the ball where you want.
   c. Feel yourself making good contact.
   d. Feed your mind with confident, positive thoughts
   e. Repeat your Cue Word (Chapter 2) if you use one.

5. **Trust Your Skills**
   a. Relax (take deep breaths if needed to help relax your body).
   b. Have your plan and then just do it
   c. Train yourself to see the ball and react instead of over-thinking during your at bat.
   d. Trust helps you get out of your own way.

**EXERCISE:** Create a pre-action routine to start using in practice. Once it becomes a habit, start applying during competition.

## C. Goals

Last but not least is the importance of establishing challenging yet realistic goals. We all need to know where we want to go with our sport and how we will get there. A "goal" without a plan is a wish. Set your goals and then write out a plan. In addition to long term goals, successful athletes have daily goals. When you show up to practice with the intent to specifically get better at something, you are preparing yourself more than by just showing up to practice.

**EXERCISE:** Set a new goal for each practice/training session. After each one, evaluate yourself on how you did. The next practice build on the day before. Ideally, the daily goals tie into your long-term goals.

***

Although most athletes prepare mentally, most neglect to follow a consistent routine. Again, there is no right or wrong way to prepare. The important thing is to be diligent about finding what works for you and being consistent with it. When we leave things to chance, it is harder to consistently reach our goals. Mental preparation requires planning and commitment.

Below, are 2 different examples to ensure that you are incorporating all 5 areas in your preparation. The first one can be used for preparation for an upcoming competition, while the second one is a daily checklist for preparation. Remember that proper preparation prevents poor performance!

## 1. Mental Game Plans

This game plan is a tool I put together to help individuals as well as teams think ahead and prepare for their upcoming competition. Using the example below, list the name of the person you are dedicating the competition to (refer to the Emotional Preparation section at the beginning of this chapter). In the next section, write down what you need to specifically do under each area of preparation. Finally, list techniques you will use to help you under each area.

*Table 1: Example of a Mental Game Plan*

| |
|---|
| **Who Packed Your Parachute?** <br> *My high school coach who believed in me despite others doubts.* <br><br> **Prepare – Release the Emergency Brake** <br>     **Emotional Preparation:** <br>     ○ *Ditch the demons by leaving all outside concerns off the court* <br>     ○ *Send my high school coach a text dedicating the game to him* <br><br>     **Technical/Tactical Preparation** <br>     ○ *Review the new plays, put in for this game* <br>     ○ *Get up 100 shots tomorrow morning* |

### Equipment Preparation:
- *Pack my bag tonight making sure I have extra socks and shoes*
- *Have energy bar available for halftime*

### Physical Preparation:
- *Make sure I am in bed by 10:00 pm*
- *Eat my normal meal the night before a game*
- *Increase water intake*
- *Stretch before going to bed and in morning*
- *Make sure I am in training room by 5:00pm*

### Mental Preparation:
- *Tonight, visualize myself running through our plays*
- *Visualize myself hitting shots from various spots on the floor*
- *Visualize how it will feel when we win*
- *Listen to my Success Script (discussed in Chapter 6)*
- *Allow enough time before the game to go through my mental game warm-up*

## Fight to The Finish-
### Start Strong
- *Make sure I have prepared the above so I am ready to start from the beginning*

o  *Start with strong body language*

o  *Repeat my "I am ..." statement*

**Refuel Mind & Body When on the Bench or in Between Plays/Point**

o  *Make sure I am "T-N-T ing" (Chapter 3) with all teammates*

o  *Keeping a vision of what I want to happen*

o  *Continue talking the talk & walking the walk*

o  *Take deep breaths*

**Finish Stronger**

o  *Ensure I am staying inside my "Me Circle" (Chapter 6)*

o  *Make sure my mind and body are strong through my talk and walk*

2. **Preparation Game Plan**

A preparation game plan is basically a check sheet for you to follow to ensure that you are preparing in all areas. The following table is an example of a game plan that I used with a college soccer team.

**Table 2:    Preparation Game Plan**

| Emotional | M | T | W | TH | F | Sat | Sun |
|---|---|---|---|---|---|---|---|
| Park issues outside field/court | | | | | | | |
| Remind yourself how lucky you are to play the game you love | | | | | | | |
| Dedicating competition | | | | | | | |
| *Add your own:* | | | | | | | |
| **Technical/Tactical** | | | | | | | |
| Know the game plan | | | | | | | |
| Know your role in the game plan | | | | | | | |
| Extra skill work | | | | | | | |
| *Add own:* | | | | | | | |
| **Equipment** | | | | | | | |
| Racquets strung/balls | | | | | | | |

| | | | | | | | |
|---|---|---|---|---|---|---|---|
| pumped/clubs clean, etc. | | | | | | | |
| Uniforms/practice gear ready to go | | | | | | | |
| Water/food available | | | | | | | |
| *Add own:* | | | | | | | |
| **Physical** | | | | | | | |
| Eating to fuel body | | | | | | | |
| Proper treatment (icing, seeing trainer, etc.) | | | | | | | |
| Stretching | | | | | | | |
| Hydrating | | | | | | | |

| | | | | | | | |
|---|---|---|---|---|---|---|---|
| Conditioning body | | | | | | | |
| *Add own:* | | | | | | | |
| **Mental** | | | | | | | |
| Mental warm-up | | | | | | | |
| Visualizing | | | | | | | |

| | | | | | | | |
|---|---|---|---|---|---|---|---|
| Talking the talk | | | | | | | |
| Walking the walk | | | | | | | |
| Staying in your Me Circle | | | | | | | |
| *Add own:* | | | | | | | |

**EXERCISE:** Create your own preparation game plan. Use the example above if needed but make sure you include specific items that help you prepare.

**Note:** *this exercise isn't helpful for all but if you are an athlete that doesn't prepare sufficiently, creating your own plan can only help, which leads to increased confidence.*

\*\*\*

*"Preparation is the cornerstone of confidence,*
*which in turn is the cornerstone of success.*
*You know what you are training for and you prepare*
*accordingly physically and mentally. A level of calm comes*
*from knowing that you've done that."*
*-Craig Alexander*

\*\*\*

In summary, when you incorporate all 5 areas of preparation, you will be ready to perform leaving little to chance. Most of us only prepare sufficiently in 2-3 of these areas, but the most successful athletes look for every possible way to gain an edge. The best athletes in their respective sports are known for their thorough preparation. Tom Brady at age 40, attributes his continued success to how well he prepares himself in these 5 areas.

The importance of preparation cannot be stated enough. It's the easiest but often most neglected area that we have 100% control over. If you take care of the little things and prepare your body daily, you will be mentally and physically more prepared and the emergency brakes will release. Make sure you leave nothing to chance! Victory loves careful preparation! Get to preparing!

*"One important key to success is self-confidence.*
*An important key to self-confidence is preparation."*
*-Arthur Ashe*

# Coaches Corner

- Create opportunities for athletes to learn by doing. Even if they are doing it wrong but working to overcome it, this prepares them and builds their confidence more than just being told what to do.

- Prepare your athletes by creating opportunities for them to learn through problem solving and overcoming adversity; overcoming adversity is good for confidence building.

- Encourage and give your athletes guidelines on how to prepare their bodies (rest, nutrition, recovery, stretching, etc.)

- Get your athletes as physically fit as you can (don't put it on them- too many won't do it).

- Give your athletes adequate time to mentally prepare and switch gears to practice as well as competitive mode.

# 6
# Talk, Walk, See, & Prepare

*"Control the Controllables"*

Mastering only one of these four skills, still keeps you on the confidence roller coaster. Getting stronger at 2-3 of them, increases your confidence. However, putting all 4 together will enable you to achieve a steady level of confidence that will stay strong in the face of any circumstance.

When teaching confidence to teams, I will often use the following exercise to drive home the importance of all four skills.

**EXERCISE** (for teams): Divide the team into 4 groups and give each group one of the steps of confidence. Allow the groups 5 minutes to discuss and plan how to convince the other groups that their area of confidence is more important than the others. Then, one group at a time stands and explains the argument for their area. After each group has gone, allow rebuttals to comments made by other groups.

It is interesting to see how often the athletes have to use another group's area to get their point across. Without fail, someone eventually makes a comment along the lines that you need all 4. Which is exactly the main point.

Coaches can add to the exercise by making it competitive and see who has the best argument. Give points each time a group makes an outstanding comment. Have a reward for the team that wins.

As I have mentioned repeatedly, the key is to consistently apply these 4 things whether things are going your way or not. **Consistent application creates a steady supply of confidence.**

\*\*\*

Another helpful activity that drives home the point of the importance of all 4 is the **Me Circle.** The Me Circle is a great visual to help athletes stay focused on what they can control. Staying focused on the controllables has a strong correlation to increased confidence.

**EXERCISE** (Note: *The directions below are for a team, but this exercise is still effective for individuals. I encourage all individuals to create their own Me Circle*):

Everyone has a sheet of paper and a writing utensil. Have each person draw a circle on their paper (it can be as big as they choose). Allow them 5-10 minutes to write inside the circle, everything in their sport that they can control 100%. Then, on the outside of the circle list things they cannot control 100%.

If leading this, you can start with a few examples. Ask them if they can control scoring. Allow for discussion, but the answer is ultimately no. For example, in basketball, all you can control is how you shoot and the shot you took. But what happens after it leaves you, is out of your control. You can't control a defender making a great defensive play. You may have scored a goal, but the ref may call a foul away from the ball. In soccer, some uncontrollables for an offensive player are: a defender making an amazing tackle; the goalie making an incredible save; or a phantom offsides call could be made. Weather conditions and officials are uncontrollable.

Example:

## "Me Circle"

**100% within my control**

Examples: Effort, focus & attitude

**Not 100% within my control**

Examples: Winning, scoring & teammates

Follow up that question, by asking them if they can control winning or losing. Allow for discussion but again the answer is no. You can't control how good your opponent is. And let's be honest, some teams or individuals are just that much better. You can't control how your teammates will perform that day, or the coaches' decisions, or the referee's calls.

As you discuss these 2 examples, you may get comments such as, "I can control how I respond or the shot I take though." Remind your athletes that those controllables go inside the Me Circle.

Let them take a few minutes to continue the activity on their own. Then, as a team, call out things outside the Me Circle. When those are exhausted, list the ones inside the circle. Confidence is center stage inside the circle. Basically, all we can control are our thoughts, our body language, how we respond (which is a combination of self-talk and body language), how we prepare our bodies, our teams, our minds. In addition, we can control our communication and our decisions but not our coaches or teammates.

We can never be truly confident, when we focus on things outside the Me Circle. You naturally gain confidence when your thoughts and energy stay focused on things within your control. Don't give away important energy and waste emotions on things you can't control. The more we can learn to stay inside the Me Circle, the more our confidence, happiness, and chance for success increases.

The best practice is to determine your baseline number. Subjectively come up with a percentage of your thoughts and energy that you feel are consistently inside the Me Circle. From there, your goal is to try to improve 1-5% each day or week. A small increase will provide big results.

*Note: Not even the best athletes in the world are 100% inside the Me Circle. Don't set yourself up for failure by being disappointed when you aren't 100% focused on what you can control. The idea is to become more aware and therefore focused on your controllables versus your uncontrollables.*

**Success Script**- A success script is akin to creating your own motivational speech that highlights your strengths and goals. It can be used as a pre-game warm-up or as an additional confidence boost. By reading or listening to it before practice or competitions, you are making sure you are programing positive/productive self-thoughts so that you start with a tank full of confidence. The idea is to plant visions of success.

**EXERCISE**:  Use the directions and example below to write your own success script. I would suggest creating one for the entire season and making minor changes to fit different competitions.

**Directions:**

- Write down your strengths, reasons you have to be confident, and your goals.
    - Your strengths (Ex. great defender, good leader, enthusiastic).
    - Past successes (Ex. having the game winner last game, milestones you have reached).
    - How you want to feel pre-game (Ex. confident, positive, ready to go).
    - Positive and productive self-talk (Ex. "this is good" attitude, "I am..." statements).
    - Your cue word that evokes a confident mindset (Ex. money, dominate, swish).
    - Key points for success (Ex. strategically, technically).
    - Use all of your senses (Ex. sights, sounds, movements, feelings, etc.).
    - A play-by-play mental image of key moments (Ex. the start, overcoming adversity, end of game situations, the finish).
    - Make sure you are talking the talk by using confident statements.

- Write in the first person- "I am...:", "I believe..."

- If you have the ability to add background music to your script, make sure it creates the mood of how you want to feel. Keep the recording short (3-5 min.) so it is easy to listen to.

- For best effect, recite it aloud in front of the mirror or if you have recorded it listen to it regularly for a confidence boost.

- As you listen to it, make sure you have strong body language and that you visualize yourself in action.

***Example of a Success Script Exercise:***
The following success script was written by an athlete competing in their nation's Olympic trials.

*As I stand on the court getting ready for the tryout to begin, I remember why I am here and why I belong.*
*I am one of the top athletes in my country. I am here because of the work I have put into basketball.*
*My confidence and enthusiasm fuels me as well as those around me.*
*I am an outstanding shooter and a great defender.*
*I am an excellent passer.*
*My willingness to put it on the line makes me a strong competitor.*
*I am completely invested in the game.*
*I belong here because I have been a starter for four years in college.*
*I have already played against the best in the US and found success.*

*I can score in a variety of ways.*

*I can take over a game when I need to.*

*I am a lockdown defender.*

*I belong here because I will out-work and out-compete anyone.*

*I belong here because I have earned it. I have never taken the short cut. The hours of preparation and hard work are what got me here.*

*I have made sacrifice after sacrifice so that I would be a better player.*

*I have earned the right to be here. I have paid my dues. I belong here.*

*The national team coaches believe I am good enough.*

*I belong here because people never believed that I would or could be as good as I am, and yet, I am not even close to being as good as I know I will be.*

*As I put on my ankle braces and lace up my shoes, I have no doubt that I belong.*

*I feel relaxed and ready to have fun, ready to compete, and be tough and aggressive. I am ready to get out and play my kind of game. I am ready to dominate.*

*I feel confident. My touch feels good on my shot. My legs feel explosive and powerful. I am full of energy.*

*I see myself playing with and connecting with my teammates; being a leader through my voice and action.*

*My focus is on the play in front of me. I easily forget about my past mistakes and errors and move forward to the next play.*

*I am in the zone. My shot is smooth and my passes crisp.*

*I am aggressive on defense; my feet are moving to stay in front of my man.*

*I am running plays to perfect execution.*
*I am in the zone. I belong here. This is my day.*

\*\*\*

When we focus on what we can control and stop wasting energy on what we can't control, our confidence grows. Preparing ourselves by talking, walking, and seeing is under our control and will pay dividends.

\*\*\*

Self-doubt is human nature. We all have it. It's just a matter of degree and determination. Confidence comes to those who fight through the self-doubt, rather than giving in to it. It comes to those that are willing to treat it as a skill that needs daily practice.

Events don't cause you to have or not have confidence. It's how you feel about them and how you react to them that determines your confidence. The key to controlling how you feel about an experience is your talk, your walk, and your vision of what you want. When you put these 3 things together and you have prepared adequately, you will control how you feel about an experience.

Building and maintaining confidence, requires you to work consistently at talking the talk, walking the walk, seeing what you want to achieve, and preparing yourself in all areas. Confidence grows once you realize that you can control only that which you have the ability to control. Having the discipline to work on these 4 things each day is the key to releasing our confidence emergency brake.

Building your confidence is like building a house. You can't do it with just one brick- but you start with one brick. Then you add another and so on, until your house is built. Your confidence works the same way. Start small and build on every success, add strong self-talk, and body language and use visualizations. Focus on what you can control until it becomes a habit and each day your confidence will improve.

Yes, you will have to work on it every day, the rewards will outweigh the hard work. Stay strong and get to building, so you can release your emergency brake!

*"Each tiny effort builds on the next,*
*so that brick by brick, magnificent things can be created."*
*-Robin Sharma*

# About the Author

Tami Matheny is Owner and Director of Refuse2LoseCoaching, LLC and Co-Owner of Success for Teams, LLC. As a certified Mental Game Coach, she works with coaches, athletes, and teams to improve areas such as confidence, focus, motivation, mental toughness, leadership, teamwork, etc.

Matheny has a passion for sports and how the mental game affects performance. As an athlete, coach, administrator and now Mental Game Coach, she has seen first-hand the difference mental toughness coupled with physical training, translates into individual and/or team success.

In high school, Tami was a tennis and basketball standout at East Rutherford High School (NC). She graduated from Lenoir-Rhyne College with a degree in psychology, while playing basketball and tennis, and earned a master's degree in sports administration from the University of North Carolina.

Prior to becoming a Mental Game Coach, Matheny was one of the most successful tennis coaches in USC Upstate tennis history and elevated the men's and women's programs to levels never seen before. With the implementation of her "Mental Toughness Program, both Spartans tennis programs produced nationally ranked individuals and teams, conference championships, and numerous individual awards. She is one of few female coaches in the nation named Conference Coach of the Year for a men's sport.

Tami has worked with various recreational, club, high school and collegiate individuals and teams in numerous sports. She has been a part of many state championships, conference championships, and a National Championship.

When not training others, Tami resides in Moore, SC and remains physically active. She has completed a handful of marathons, including the Boston Marathon and ultramarathons. Her longest race to date is a 40 miler. She is an avid cyclist, completing rides over 80 miles. Matheny continues to seek new mental and physical challenges. Connect with Tami on twitter @R2LCoaching or @Tamimatheny

# Confidence Resources

*Use social media to build confidence and mindsets.

*Follow "The Confident Athlete" on twitter @tamimatheny and Refuse2LoseCoaching @r2lcoaching

## June '20 — The Confident Calendar

| Start Strong Sunday | Make a Difference Monday | Talk the Talk Tuesday | Walk the Walk Wednesday | Thankful Thursday | Focused Friday | See it, Be it Saturday |
|---|---|---|---|---|---|---|
| | 1. Say Something Nice Day What we say to others can make a big difference in their day and life. | 2. Say what you want to happen vs what you fear will happen. | 3. Become intentional about your body movements. This can build self-confidence. | 4. "THIS IS GOOD: A Journey on Overcoming Adversity" Release Date! | 5. Find the "This is Good" http://r2lc.com/20 20/03/23/this-is-good-2/ | 6. We aren't limited to what our eyes can see, but by what our minds can see. |
| 7. Recognition of success builds confidence. Make sure to celebrate your successes. | 8. Send a specific text to a teammate or friend to boost their confidence. | 9. Self-talk is the most powerful form of communication. It either propels you or pulls you back. | 10. T-N-T Talk & Touch with all teammates to build connection and confidence. | 11. Practicing gratitude is like doing sit-ups. We're training our brains to focus on the positive. | 12. Focus on being a thermostat instead of a thermometer. | 13. Acts of Light Day "There are two ways of spreading light; to be the candle or the mirror that reflects it." ~ Edith Wharton |
| 14. List all the reasons you have to be confident. Review the list occasionally and add to. | 15 National Smile Power Day Focus on how many smiles you can give & the power that it gives you to make a difference. | 16. Change self-talk by: Recognize it. Stop it. Reframe it to positive or productive self-talk. | 17. Body language influences the way others feel around you. | 18. Successful people are thankful for their opportunities and blessings. | 19. Focus on your relationships. R'ships > C'chips. | 20. Summer Begins Take time today to see where you really are and where you want to go. |
| 21. Father's Day Take time to honor and thank the dad's that play a role in your life. | 22. Give Back Today. Consistently giving back creates a really good feeling. This feeds confidence. | 23. Create "we are…" statements for your team. | 24. Wear Your Confidence Today! Head up, shoulders back, smile on! | 25. Start each morning by thinking & speaking about all the things you are thankful for today. | 26. What you focus on grows. | 27. A tiger doesn't lose sleep over the opinion of sheep. What's important is how you see yourself, not how others do. |
| 28. Confidence comes before competence. Anchor your confidence in the belief that you will get better as you put in the work. | 29. Confident people make everyone around them better. Cocky people try to look better than others. | 30. Get rid of "don't." Your brain doesn't recognize the word "don't." So, you still end up picturing whatever you said "don't" about. | Confidence comes from taking daily action! | Twitter: @tamimatheny @r2lcoaching Instagram: @refuse2losecoaching Email: tami@r2lc.com | All books available on Amazon. | |

If you would like to receive next month's Confidence Calendar go to www.r2lc.com and click on the link at the bottom

*Subscribe to our Monthly Confidence Calendar. Go to www.r2lc.com and subscribe at the bottom of the page.

*Contact tami@r2lc.com and schedule an in person or zoom session for your team.

# Other Books by Tami Matheny

## "This is Good: A Journey on Overcoming Adversity"

 Adversity is often seen as a bad thing. Something to avoid. But to accomplish anything worthwhile adversity is necessary. It is what separates the great from the mediocre, the champions from the contenders. The difference is in how you look at adversity. Success comes from learning to see it, think about it, and respond to it in a positive or productive way. Creating a "this is good" mindset will allow you to do this.

## "The Confidence Journal"

 A combination of a daily journal and a confidence resource. Each page gives you a new thought, quote, or tip on confidence. The rest of the page is for your thoughts. A great tool for a journey toward greater confidence in all you do.

Both are available on Amazon.
Contact tami@r2lc.com for group pricing.

Made in the USA
Monee, IL
25 January 2023

26276501R00066